D0899258

WITHDRAWN FROM COLLECTION OF
SACRAMENTO PUBLIC LIBRARY

Puppies

Julie Murray

Abdo
BABY ANIMALS
Kids

abdopublishing.com

Published by Abdo Kids, a division of ABDO, PO Box 398166, Minneapolis, Minnesota 55439.
Copyright © 2018 by Abdo Consulting Group, Inc. International copyrights reserved in all countries.
No part of this book may be reproduced in any form without written permission from the publisher.

Printed in the United States of America, North Mankato, Minnesota.

052017

092017

THIS BOOK CONTAINS
RECYCLED MATERIALS

Photo Credits: iStock, Shutterstock

Production Contributors: Teddy Borth, Jennie Forsberg, Grace Hansen

Design Contributors: Christina Doffing, Candice Keimig, Dorothy Toth

Publisher's Cataloging in Publication Data

Names: Murray, Julie, 1969-, author.

Title: Puppies / by Julie Murray.

Description: Minneapolis, Minnesota : Abdo Kids, 2018 | Series: Baby animals |
     Includes bibliographical references and index.

Identifiers: LCCN 2016962327 | ISBN 9781532100062 (lib. bdg.) |
     ISBN 9781532100758 (ebook) | ISBN 9781532101304 (Read-to-me ebook)

Subjects: LCSH: Puppies--Juvenile literature. | Puppies--Infancy--Juvenile
     literature.

Classification: DDC 636.7--dc23

LC record available at http://lccn.loc.gov/2016962327

Table of Contents

Puppies

A baby dog is a puppy.

A litter often has 3 to 8 puppies.

Puppies cannot see at birth.

They cannot hear either.

They sleep and eat.

They drink their mother's milk.

Puppies want to move. They can walk at 3 weeks old.

They love to play!

A puppy can be adopted at

8 weeks old.

Kayla cuddles her Labrador.

She loves her puppy!

Watch a Border Collie Grow!

newborn

6 weeks

12 weeks

1 year

Glossary

adopt
to become the owner and
caretaker of a pet.

litter
a number of young produced at
one birth by a mammal.

Index

abdokids.com

Use this code to log on to abdokids.com and access crafts, games, videos, and more!

Abdo Kids Code:
BPK0062

24